ETIQUETTE

HANDBOOK

Everything you need to know about etiquette condensed into a small and easy to read handbook

by Valentina Palermo V.

CHAPTERS

INTRODUCTION

Etiquette is a topic that has been around for thousands of years, even if it didn't have the same name back then. Even people in ancient Rome had a certain code of behaviour that indicated who was part of the elite.

What I'm looking to achieve with this book is to give you a complete introduction to etiquette as well as easily memorable rules to follow in any situation so you're always prepared. This handbook is perfect if you're a person who doesn't like wasting time but wants to learn a valuable skill. Etiquette is present in more aspects of our lives than we notice and as long as we have company we will be watched and observed, some companies even take you out for dinner or lunch to examine you! Luckily, you'll invest less than an hour of your valuable time reading this and you'll be prepared to impress the incredulous with your good manners and charming presence. The book itself is divided into areas so you have easy access to the topic you're looking to find information on.

As you may imagine, it would be virtually impossible to summarise each and every rule of etiquette worth knowing in such a short book, however, I know if I wrote a 500-page book filled with every single detail you wouldn't memorise (or even read) it entirely. This short handbook includes (almost) everything you need to know about etiquette in order to be well prepared for the real world ranging from topics such as tact to social media to being invited to sleep over at a friend's house.

I hope you find the contents of this book valuable and easy to read, understand and implement into your daily life. I went to my first etiquette course when I was around 15 and I absolutely loved it! One of the reasons why etiquette captured my interest is how intricate it is. There are hundreds of rules to follow and memorise it's almost ridiculous. I have used these rules countless times and let me tell you, the more you practice using them, the easier it becomes.

Disclaimer: Etiquette rules vary from place to place but I'll do my best to cover as much as possible and find the most useful amount of information for the general readers.

WHAT THE F*** IS ETIQUETTE

Probably the thing that holds you back from using the f-word as often as you'd like. If you're more of a definition type of person, let me put it into words. According to the Cambridge dictionary, etiquette is the set of <u>rules</u> or <u>customs</u> that <u>control</u> <u>accepted</u> <u>behaviour</u> in <u>particular</u> <u>social</u> <u>groups</u> or <u>social</u> <u>situations</u>. In other words, it's the proper way to behave. Us human beings are social beings by nature, this means that you will have to participate in social interactions with other human beings on a daily basis. Many people consider etiquette to be a branch of decorum or general social behaviour. In other words, it is the socially accepted behaviour or the rules of conduct. Each society has its own distinct etiquette and various cultures within a society also have their own rules and social norms. Learning these codes of behaviour can be very challenging for people who are new to a particular culture. Let's say you go to Argentina and someone tries to kiss you on the cheek to say hello while you are only offering a handshake. Rude (and rather intrusive)! Well, that's how people usually say hello in Latin America.

The rules of etiquette dictate how people behave. Taking the last example, the concept of greeting people politely and with respect is common to the codes of behaviour of many cultures, even though the way in which that respect is expressed varies a lot from region to region. In some Asian countries, people may bow or clasp their hands together when greeting someone, while in the United Stated people often shake hands or hug each other if they are close like family or friends.

It is safe to assume that there is an etiquette role for pretty much every situation one might encounter, from meeting the President of the United States to politely declining a meal in the Middle East. Since the social norms of different cultures are so different, many people (and I would strongly encourage this as well) study etiquette before travelling or entering a new social circle to ensure that they do not cause offence or embarrass themselves. It is also very important to not get offended or take it as a personal insult if a person behaves under their own code, they may not know it's different where you are.

The consequences of mistakes in etiquette may vary. It could go from someone feeling slightly awkward and making the people present at the time of the mistake form an unfavourable impression of the offender to a bigger mistake causing the loss of a friendship or job. In some countries and regions, a serious breach could even cost you time in jail or even your life. Even though this example is a bit extreme, it does apply in some parts of the world. Depending on where you are and who you are with, some people might be happy to answer questions or help you with guidance about basic etiquette before you enter a certain situation. If you do make a mistake, don't be afraid to apologise, most people accept apologies, especially when they're made promptly and it also shows you're aware of your mistake and willing to correct it.

ARE MANNERS AND ETIQUETTE THE SAME THING?

Etiquette and manners are not the same things, although they're quite alike. Let me explain. In order to answer this question, we first need to define what each one of these words means. According to the Cambridge Dictionary, Etiquette is "the set of rules or customs that control accepted behaviour in particular social groups or social situations". Keyword being accepted behaviour. While Manners are "ways of behaving toward people, esp. ways that are socially correct and show respect for their comfort and their feelings". Having good manners is the root of etiquette while having etiquette may just be a mask of manners. Put into other words, manners are kindness, whereas etiquette is simply an organised way of doing things such as setting the table and sitting the guests.

Etiquette comes out of manners, whose intentions are to develop an organised, orderly system of doing things, taking into consideration how those actions might affect others. Therefore, it is possible for someone to have etiquette but not real manners. Just like someone may do and say all the right things but you still feel that there is something not right, it could be a facade.

For example, it is etiquette to stand to the right (or left, depending where you're from) on an escalated so that people who are in a hurry can pass you quickly without disturbing someone else. If you do not think of others and stand wherever you want, the other person will be unable to pass you without discomfort and lose time. Now, it's not like we've always positioned ourselves that way in the escalator, etiquette is a system that develops over time. If we never spent a second thinking about why everyone moves to the side of the escalator we would then have etiquette, not manners. The "thinking about others" part is manners while the social behaviour of moving towards the corner is etiquette. Ideally, we should have both good manners and etiquette. Manners have their root in kindness. Once you are kind, thoughtful and considerate of others, you won't have to do much effort to memorise the rules of etiquette. That is generally speaking of course, we should make some effort to learn about general etiquette or the etiquette of another culture, especially if we have friends from other cultures. This is quite useful if you're required to work in another country or if you travel often.

Now, is it possible for someone to have good manners but not etiquette? Of course. As wonderful as we like to think we are, we have different ways of being thoughtful. We also have different ways of interpreting kindness and thoughtfulness. If we offer an older adult our seat, we are acting in kindness. If the elderly person takes it the wrong way and thinks that you are labelling him or her old, then our action in his or her mind is not an act of kindness. These differences are more apparent in culture. Each culture has developed its own social behaviour and thus etiquette. Another example is learning the dining etiquette of various cuisines. You may have the best intentions in the world but still offend a hostess by pouring the wrong sauce over your food or giving the wrong present. Just as in some Asian cultures the giving of clocks is similar to "wishing death upon them" or shoes to say their relationship won't last, giving a shirt as a gift could feel too personal if you don't know that person so well.

When you visit homes, in some cultures it is polite to offer to help wash up the dishes, while in others, helping to wash the dishes is an intrusion of privacy. These are all etiquette, not manners. We can reach the conclusion that manners go first and etiquette goes second. It's more important to make the people around you feel comfortable than to follow the rules all the time.

THE IMPORTANCE OF ETIQUETTE

Etiquette serves several important functions in today's world. One of them is that it provides personal security and confidence. Knowing how to behave appropriately in a given situation makes you feel more comfortable. I have been in some situations in which I wasn't sure how to act and it's not the best feeling. If you find yourself in a situation like this you can always try to imitate the people who are there with you.

Behaving appropriately also protects the feelings of others. Proper etiquette requires that you make others comfortable and don't hurt their feelings. You should not point out their errors or draw attention to their mistakes. If they do something wrong it is better to ignore or pretend you didn't notice it and continue the conversation. I have more than enough personal examples for this particular topic but I'm grateful my dates have always been gentlemen who spared me the embarrassment and didn't bring it up.

It makes communication clearer since etiquette enhances communication by breaking down barriers, not erecting them.

It enhances your status at work since in any working situation you are perceived as more capable, more professional and more intelligent if you are familiar with the proper code of conduct for the workplace.

Lastly and probably the most important, it makes a good first impression. Always remember that there is no second chance to make a first impression. The first five to seven seconds after you meet someone is crucial. Your first impression lingers in the other person's mind long after you're gone. If you use proper etiquette, that first impression will most likely be a positive one. First impressions rely a lot on visuals as well so be sure to always look clean and presentable.

Society and cultures are changing so fast that it is hard for rules of etiquette to keep up. Keep in mind that etiquette is meant to be a guideline, not a set of strict rules carved in stone. Those guidelines are developed using common sense, a sense of fairness, politeness and, above all, consideration for others. If you let consideration for others be your final arbiter, you will be well on your way to being the kind of polite person who understands the rules of etiquette instinctively.

THE BASICS OF ETIQUETTE

There are several guidelines to be considered as the basics of etiquette, if you can master this you are already halfway there. Your manners are always on display, make it a goal to leave a good impression. Being courteous and respectful towards others is essential. Many etiquette experts share the opinion that following the Golden Rule of "treating others the way you would like to be treated" is best when interacting with people. Here are the guidelines:

- Make an effort to be considerate to others. Holding the door open for the person behind you or not having one person save a space in line or at a theatre for 10 other people are exhibitions of consideration. Arrive on time for events to avoid bumping and crawling over people. If you must pass over those who are seated, say "excuse me" and pass facing the person. It is better to see one's face than their back side.
- Do not allow your behaviour to disturb others. Keep your feet on the floor and not on the seats around you. When talking, keep your voice low or wait until intermissions and between performances. Don't draw attention to yourself bu shouting loud comments or booing performers. At concerts, refrain from singing along or humming unless asked by the performer or when at a concert in which is common to do so. Don't talk on the phone (loudly or for too long) or listen to music out loud if you're surrounded by other people and the place is quiet. People don't want to hear if your gossip and they are most likely not into the same music as you. Bring headphones and keep the call short, you can always text if it's something important. Similar to this is talking to other people in a public place. If you're communicating with the person right in front of you,

screaming is not necessary. Be considerate and keep the conversation sound at a normal level.

- Always play it safe when drinking. If you are having a good time and alcohol is involved, ask someone in your party to be the designated driver beforehand. It is important that everyone enjoys themselves responsibly. Don't drink too much, if you are starting to feel tipsy, switch your drink for water. Avoid using social media during this period as you might post something you will regret in the morning.

- Follow the established rules of any venue you are in. If food and drink are not allowed, don't sneak it in. If it is allowed, clean up your area before leaving and properly discard trash. Always sit in your assigned seat.

- When sneezing in public you should always (and I mean it, always) cover your mouth. Other people don't want to be covered in your germs, just like you wouldn't want to be covered in theirs. Don't pick your nose or blow your nose too loudly.

- Regarding personal hygiene, never leave your house if you know you smell, you can always take a quick shower, change your clothes, wash your teeth or (as a last resort) spray yourself with deodorant or perfume. If you just notice this and you're out and about you can ask friends or coworkers for mints or deodorant. It is a good idea to bring deodorant, wipes, mouth wash, mints, tissues, perfume and even a change of clothes with you just in case, you can leave your essentials kit in your car if you want and only use as necessary. You should also take special care of your looks, people can notice when you haven't washed your face or if your clothes have a hole in them or are dirty.

- Cover your mouth when you yawn and don't make it too exaggerated either. Try to refrain from yawning or make it as least noticeable as possible when talking to someone as they will perceive it as a sign you're bored or not entertained by them.

- Chew with your mouth closed and don't talk unless you have swallowed. We don't want to see that half-chewed food inside your mouth, it's not very appealing. When using cutlery, start from the outside and work your way in. The big glasses are for water and red wine, wait for the waiter to serve the beverages if you don't know which one is for what. If you order a bottle of wine and they give you the cork, don't smell it, just look at it. Don't cover your wine or water glasses in smudges, drink from only one place and grab the glass by its stem. I'll expand these topics in a later chapter.
- In regard to swearing: We all know that person who swears a f*** ton but do we know what type of effect this has on other people? People who swear are considered more honest but that's because they don't moderate what they are talking about. Most commonly it is not quite well seen or received and it produces a negative reaction on the people you're talking to. However, the acceptability of this is also linked with where you are located geographically as well as the place and context you're using the word in. Moderate your language if you're in an elegant place or in front of children. I would suggest avoiding this (at least for this context of etiquette) as it's not perceived as classy or educated.
- When sitting you can cross your legs in most situations. If you are a lady in an elegant place it is suggested that you cross one ankle over the other. Refrain from crossing your legs at church. Keep your posture straight and do not sit with your legs wide open.
- You should always respond to an invitation as soon as possible, some people rely on your response in order to make decisions for the event, they could even invite another person if you can't attend or postpone the event if many invitees can't go. To accept or decline an invitation, you should always express gratefulness for being invited and then give your answer. You could say something like: "Thank you so much for inviting me to

your celebration, I am deeply sorry I won't be able to attend but I wish you the best on your special day."
- When receiving gifts you should always thank the person who sent you the gift as soon as you get it, even if you did not like the gift. You can do this in person, via phone call or even by a message. The message doesn't need to be long and it goes a long way. "Thank you so much for the gift you gave me, I look forward to using it!" or "The wine you brought to the dinner was amazing, thank you so much for the detail."
- When giving someone a gift you should take into consideration the other person's preferences, needs and style. Even if you are sure the other person will like the gift you are giving them it is a nice gesture to include the receipt they give you in order to change what you've purchased.
- Gifting money can be a delicate topic in some cultures, it is best to do this with people you know such as family or when the person specifically asks for this, such as when they state "compensation" as a gift for a wedding. It is also a nice detail if the person is going on a trip out of the country or if they are moving abroad. Take into consideration how much you are giving as well, you should try to gift an amount that's not too low and not too high.

Basically, don't do to others what you wouldn't want to be done to you. Before you do anything or if you're in doubt whether or not something is correct or acceptable, ask yourself how would you feel if the person next to you was doing it. Also, if you find yourself in a situation in which another person is doing something that's bothering you, make a mental note not to do it yourself.

Tact
I would consider tact as one of the most special abilities you could have. Mastering the ability of tact is not as easy as the other rules but it is just as important. Tact will allow

you to express yourself with elegance even when what you have to say is difficult. The best way to describe is with the words of Winston S. Churchill. "Tact is the ability to tell someone to go to hell in such a way that they look forward to the trip." I don't expect you to be a total lady or gentleman at all times, I would actually encourage you to defend yourself if the other person crosses the line. However, do it with style. It's all about how you say it, always remember that the moment you get angry by provocation is the moment you lose. Never let them win, slap them back with so much elegance they don't even notice the burn.

Wit
The first time I heard this concept I didn't quite understand it. Wit means, according to the Oxford dictionary, both "The capacity for inventive thought and quick understanding; keen intelligence" and "A natural aptitude for using words and ideas in a quick and inventive way to create humour". Use your words in a smart way, you can say almost anything when you're backed with humor. He who resorts to insults has run out of ideas. Wit is going to help you leave a charming impression in those you have met. Humour is an underrated way of earning the hearts of those we spend time with.

MEETING SOMEONE FOR THE FIRST TIME

If you're meeting someone for the first time, it is extremely important that you show good manners as a form of respect and politeness. Once again, the importance of the first impression comes afloat. You want them to see your best side and make the best first impression you can. Always put on a smile or have a relaxed look on your face, you don't want them to think you're not enjoying meeting them.

How to greet someone correctly depending on the area
Even though it is summarised in this chapter, you should investigate on your own before you go to a certain country so you can practise the right pronunciation and way of greeting people. If you have a friend who lives there, don't hesitate to ask them what you should say and how you should act.

North America: say "Hello". Offer a handshake if you are just meeting someone, hug if you are close to the person or if they are family.

Latin America: A friendly "hola" will cut it in most cases. "Olá" in Brazil. Kiss on the cheek unless you are a man saying hello to another man, then handshake. If it is a more professional scenario, offer a handshake to both men and women.

Asia: learn the proper way to say hello according to the country you are visiting, in some Asian countries, people bow to say hello while in others it is acceptable to offer a handshake.
Japan: say "konnichiwa" and learn to bow the right way.
China: handshake, say "ni hao".
India: say "namaste", hold your hands together as if you were praying and a slight bow.

Hong Kong: say "neih hou" or "hello".
Korea: say "Anyong Haseyo".
Thailand: if you are a man, say "sawasdee khrap" if you are a woman, say "sawasdee kha" and add a wai (hold your hands together in front of your face and bow slightly) whether you are a man or woman.

Europe: learn how to say hello in the language of the country you're visiting. Handshakes are the most common but in some countries they say hello with kisses on the cheek. Here are some examples.
Britain: "Hello"
Germany, : "Hallo"
France: "Bonjour"
Spain: "Hola"
Portugal: "Olá"
Russia: "Zdravstvuyte"
Italy: "Ciao"

Africa: each of the countries in Africa has their own way to say hello, I'd strongly advise you learn the proper way for each country before you visit. Here are some examples.
Angola, Mozambique: say "Olá"
Cameroon: say "Bonjour"
Egypt, Libya, Morocco, Sudan: say "As-Salaam-Alaikum"
Kenya: say "Jambo"
South Africa: Zulu: "Sawubona", Xhosa: "Molo",
Afrikaans: "Hallo", English: "Hello"

Australia: say "hello"

When you're casually introduced to someone, look that person in the eye, smile and offer your hand (adjust accordingly to the country). As you are shaking hands, introduce yourself and get the other person's name. Repeating the name will help you remember it. Do not forget the person's name. If you do, ask common friends quietly to get you back on track. One trick to remembering names is to use them in conversation, the more you repeat it, the easier it will stick. You can also associate it with someone you already know or a thing that makes it easy to remember. If her name is Ariel, you can associate it with the little mermaid. If his name is John, you can associate it to your uncle John or your neighbour, Johnattan.

What you can talk about
After meeting someone you can always compliment one of their traits such as their eyes or hair or one of their belongings such as their dress, bag or shoes. This will make the other person feel good and will lighten the mood. You can also talk about their profession, education, family or if they are working on any project at the moment. Always listen carefully to what they are saying, don't just wait for your turn to talk.
If you want to learn more about this topic a great book I'd recommend is How to Win Friends & Influence People by Dale Carnegie

Some topics to avoid
Don't talk about politics or religion or anything that may spark very strong feelings. You want to keep the conversation pleasant and enjoyable for all parties.

If you are in a hurry or you must go, excuse yourself, smile and tell them it's been a pleasure to meet them, followed by their name.

GOING OUT TO EAT

If you are going to share a meal with anyone it is a must to learn proper table manners. This not only speaks of your own education but also how your parents educated you and if they took the time to teach you when you were young.

There are some basic table manners which are important in both professional and social situations so it's a good idea to memorise them. There may be some slight variations depending on the region in which you're in and what is locally acceptable. This chapter is divided into two big areas which are going out to eat at a restaurant and going to someone's house. If you are at a dinner party and you don't know what to do, pay attention to the host or hostess and take cues from them. If you are at a restaurant with coworkers you can also imitate them as long as you know they behave properly.

Before the dinner

If you are invited to have dinner with someone, it is always a good idea to respond, even if an RSVP is not requested. This helps the other person plan in advance. Don's ask if you can bring extra guests if the invitation doesn't make the offer. However, if your family is invited to someone's home for dinner, it is okay to ask if your children are invited as well. If they are, make sure your children know good manners before they go.

If you're meeting someone at a restaurant for dinner, be sure to be punctual. Arriving 5-10 minutes late is still acceptable but if you are running late you should let the other person know you won't be arriving on time and at what time you will be there.

Gifts

When you're invited to a friend's home, it is an excellent idea to bring the host or hostess a gift. Don't expect your gift to be used during the meal, most dinner parties have carefully planned the menu and your gift may not go with the meal. Some of the gifts you can bring are wine, chocolate or something you know the hosts will enjoy. Do not bring something that might make the hosts uncomfortable or cause them stress.

You don't have to worry about bringing a gift to a restaurant, however be sure to be in a good mood and act like a pleasant companion.

Getting started

Some dinner parties are formal and have cards with your name placed where the host or hostess wants you to sit. If there aren't any, ask if there are seating preferences. If you are shy, wait for others to sit or go to their place. Wait until the host sits before you do. In some cultures, a blessing will be said before starting the meal. Even if you don't follow the beliefs of the prayer, show respect and be silent. If the host offers a toast, lift your glass. It is not necessary to "clink" someone else's glass and if you do "clink" make sure it is not too strong.

Once you sit down, keep everything off the table that doesn't absolutely need to be there. This includes purses, keys, and your elbows.

Cell phones

You might feel the need to answer your phone whenever someone is calling or texting you but when you are at a meal you should always keep your phone on silent. Turn off your cell phone before sitting down and don't leave it on the table. It is rude to talk on your phone or text while in the company of others. If you're expecting an important call, leave your phone on silent and excuse yourself if you must take the call.

Napkin

As soon as you sit down, turn to your host and take a cue for when to begin. Once the host unfolds his or her napkin, you should remove your napkin from the table or plate and place it onto your lap. Use it to gentle blot your lips between bites and keep the dirty side facing the interior.

If you are dining out, you should place the napkin in your lap immediately after sitting down.

Always keep your napkin in your lap until you have finished eating. If you must get up at any time during the meal and plan to return, place the napkin on your seat unfolded. After you are finished, place the napkin on the table to the right of your plate. Do not refold your napkin, place it unfolded beside your plate. Never, under any circumstance, use your napkin as a bib.

When to eat

Just as in the last scenarios, when you are at a dinner party you should start eating when everyone has been served or when the host asks you to start.

If you are eating out, you should wait until all the members of your group have been served before actually picking up your fork. However, if you are at a buffet, you may start when there are others seated at your table. If you're going to order something from the menu remember ladies should go first.

Silverware

One of the most common issues that confuse people is which utensil to use for each course. A typical rule of thumb is to start with the one that is furthest from your plate and work your way towards the center. If you see the host or hostess doing something different, you may follow his or her lead. Glasses can also be confusing but odds are other people will be serving you the drinks. If it is a cold drink you should grab it by the thin part, this is called the stem and it keeps your hand's heat from warming up the drink.

Food
For dinners where food is served at the table, the dishes should be passed in a counter-clockwise flow. Never reach across the table for anything. Instead, ask that condiments be passed from the person closest to the item. Salt and pepper should be passed together. Always use serving utensils and not your own fork or spoon to lift food from the serving dish.

Eating
Here are some essential dining etiquette rules that are very important to follow:
- Never talk when you have food in your mouth, even if someone asks you a question. Wait until you've swallowed before answering.
- Taste your food before you add salt, pepper, or any other seasoning. This could be offending to the hosts or the chef as it is a way of saying you are not satisfied with the flavour. If salt and pepper are not provided, don't ask for them.
- Do not cut all of your food before you start eating. Cut one or two bites at a time and let the cutlery rest every now and then. Don't eat too fast as you'll look as if you haven't eaten in a while.
- Don't blow on your food. If it is hot wait a few minutes for it to cool off.
- Some foods are meant to be eaten with your fingers. These foods can be uncomfortable to eat so you should take that into consideration if you're the host.
- If you're drinking from a stemmed glass, hold it by the stem.
- Break your bread into bite-sized pieces and butter only one bite at a time.
- Try at least one or two bites of everything that's on your plate, unless you're allergic to it.

- Compliment the host or hostess if you like the food, but don't voice your opinion if you don't.
- Use your utensils for eating, be careful not to gesture with them.
- Keep your elbows off the table. Rest the arm you're not using in your lap.
- Eat slowly and pace yourself to finish at approximately the same time as the host. Don't rush through your meal, take your time to cut your food into bite-sized pieces and chew thoroughly. Don't put another bite into your mouth until you have swallowed the previous one.
- Avoid burping or making other sounds at the table.
- If you spill something at a dinner party, pick it up and blot the spill. Offer to have it professionally cleaned if necessary. If you spill something at a restaurant, signal one of the servers to help.
- When you finish eating, leave your utensils on your plate in the right position.
- Never use a toothpick or dental floss at the table even if toothpicks are available. If you have food stuck in your teeth, excuse yourself and take care of the problem in the restroom.
- Avoid grooming at the table when you're eating out, it is considered bad manners to brush or comb your hair. Don't freshen your makeup at the table, excuse yourself and go to the ladies room to do so.

Communication with servers

You must be polite with your server at all times. To be otherwise indicates bad manners. Dissatisfaction with any aspect of the food or service should be discreetly communicated to the server. If you are not happy with the response, speak to the manager. Remember that the server has no control over the quality of the food or the amount of time it takes for the kitchen staff to prepare it. If you discover a foreign object in your food such as a hair or a big, call the server to your table and quietly show him or her. There is no point in making a scene, so handle the situation as discreetly as possible.

Smoking

Very few restaurants allow smoking. However, if you are dining at a restaurant that does allow it, never smoke between courses. Wait until after the meal is over: ask if anyone objects, and if no one does then go ahead and light up. If someone at the next table appears to be bothered by your smoke, excuse yourself and finish smoking outside. Never use your plate as an ashtray. Follow the same procedure when at an acquaintance's house, ask if you can smoke inside and if not, do so outside.

Paying and tipping

If you dine in a restaurant, you should expect to tip for service. The amount you should tip varies from country to country but it's usually between 10% and 20%.

After the meal

After you finish eating, partially fold (pick by the middle to form a triangular shape) your napkin and place it to the right of your plate. Wait until the host or hostess signals that the meal is over to stand up. Don't leave immediately after the meal is over. If nothing is planned after dinner, stick around for approximately 30 minutes to an hour before saying goodbye to the host and thanking him or her for the dinner. If the event is informal, you may offer help to clean up.

Later

Always send the host or hostess a thank you note or card in the mail and don't wait for more than a day or two after the event. Address the host or hostess, thank him or her for the lovely dinner and add another short, positive comment to show your appreciation. Your note may be brief but heartfelt. You can do this over the phone or message them as well.

Going out to eat with children
It is a good idea to teach your children (or even your siblings) proper etiquette in all aspects of their lives, particularly when their manners may affect others. Start working with them as soon as you can but don't put them into situations until they are ready. Also, don't make it a stressful event for them. Children can learn really fast and the process can be fun.

There are some guidelines to follow when dining with children. If you're going to a formal restaurant, speak to the manager first. Many restaurants have special seating for families. Teach your children basic manners before going out to eat. Leave babies at home with a sitter for a more relaxed and enjoyable experience. At the first sign of a meltdown or other bad behaviour, remove your child from the dining room and take him to a calmer place. Ask him what's going on, chances are they're tired, bored or frustrated. Bring quiet activities such as colouring books, puzzles or games in your phone to entertain your child while waiting for the food to arrive.

HOSTING

If you're having someone visit for the first time, it is extremely important that you show good manners as a form of respect and politeness. The objective should be to make the other person feel as comfortable as possible. You can get ahead by following a few simple guidelines.

If you're already expecting the person, make sure you do your research. Find out more about them and get information such as their name, place of origin, occupation and reason for visiting if they're from another country. This will help you have a smoother conversation. Use this information to ask the person about where they come from or what they like to do in their free time to find common interests you can talk about. Avoid touching topics such as politics or religion (even their football team), anything that might spark strong opinions and feelings is out of boundaries as they might start heated discussions and put any or both sides in an uncomfortable position. Talking about a topic they know about will make them feel more comfortable as well as give the impression that you were anticipating their arrival or looking forward to the meeting.

Hosting a dinner

Having friends over for dinner is a fun activity which everyone should enjoy. This is the perfect way to celebrate your birthday, a holiday or an accomplishment. There are a few simple ways you can make the meeting more enjoyable.
- Send invitations at least one week in advance so people can make time for your dinner party.
- Take into consideration your guests' food preferences and if they have any allergies.
- Clean your house in advance so you are not stressed about it hours before the guests arrive. This includes

emptying the trash can and having all of your dishes and cutlery clean.
- Have everything ready so you can spend time with your guests instead of cooking.
- Set the table correctly and elegantly before your guests arrive. Use cloth napkins, these will make a good impression.
- Put on music to make the ambiance more fun and relaxing, be careful not to set it too loud.
- Welcome your guests in a relaxed mood, people can feel when you are stressed. It is allowed to have one glass of wine before they arrive, you deserve it.
- Once your guests start to arrive, offer them drinks and bring out the appetisers. You can use this as a cue to put any food that needs cooking in the oven. Make sure to set a timer and check on it from time to time.
- If one of your guests says no thank you to one of the dishes you are offering, don't force them.
- Serve dessert, you can even do so in another area designated for dessert and tea or coffee.
- Plan an activity after dinner so your guests have time to digest before they leave.
- Hire help if you have more people coming over than what you think you can manage by yourself or if the dinner is formal.
- If you need help and someone offers it, accept it. This is more to take dishes to and from the kitchen and into the dining room, not washing said dishes. Remember to thank them during and after this help is provided. If you don't want people in your kitchen, kindly decline.

All of these tips are easier said than done but be sure to enjoy yourself and don't worry too much about everything being perfect. Don't apologise if something doesn't go as planned, your guests know you can't control everything.

Hosting a sleepover
Do you have a feeling that the people who stay at your house enjoy themselves? What do you think you're doing

right and what do you think you could do better? Here are a few things you can do in order to make the experience more enjoyable for your guests:

- Welcome the people visiting in a proper way and show them where everything is, this includes, the room they will be staying in, bathroom and common area.
- Give them time to adjust, relax or change clothes if they've just arrived from a long trip.
- Let them know the agenda for the next day, if there's any and ask if they would like to adjust it in any way. Some people might want to go to the supermarket as it is common to forget essentials.
- Provide a pillow and blanket, even if they're staying on the couch. You don't want them to feel cold or uncomfortable. Most people will not ask for these things even if they want them.
- Give them the wifi password. Bonus points if you provide a USB charging point for their phones, camera o tablet.
- Make things easy to find such as towels, toilet paper, period pads, soap, toothpaste, extra toothbrush, mouthwash, razor, deodorant or anything else they might need and you can give them. They might be embarrassed to ask for any of these things so be sure to tell them they are free to use whatever they want.
- Make sure the towels and linens you provide smell fresh and are clean.
- Provide water, snacks such as nuts, fruit or granola bars, and something to read such as a book or magazine so that they don't have to leave the room or stand discomfort in the middle of the night.
- If you can, talk to your guests before they arrive and ask them if they have any food preferences or allergies and adjust accordingly. If your guests are vegan or vegetarian be sure to cater these lifestyles as well. If one of the guests surprises you with any food preferences, offer to take them to the supermarket.

- Be sure to stack up on universal food options such as cereal, oatmeal, eggs, bacon, toast, peanut butter, jam, fruit or anything else you'd like as a guest.
- If they are staying for over two days, give them space to unpack and put their clothes.

Think how would you feel if you were staying over at your house and don't forget to ask if they need anything. Make them feel comfortable at all times and they will have the best time at your place.

GUESTING

If you are the one coming over to a person's place, try to bring a little something to show respect such as a bottle of wine, truffles or a pie. Always respect the host's rules and beliefs while you are in his or her home. Here is a list of more things good guests tend to do.

- Greet the person warmly as he or she opens the door.
- Do not enter the house until you are invited in. Once you are inside, wait until you are invited to sit.
- Do not touch items and other decorations inside the house.
- Stay with the people you came in with until you are introduced to other people.
- When dining, always practice good table manners.
- Do not eat until the host has started to eat or insists that you begin first.
- You can share stories and jokes at the table as long as you consider these appropriate and decent. Avoid green jokes and other offensive remarks when meeting someone for the first time.
- Keep some of your opinions to yourself. You should think and review your possible comment before blurting it out.
- If you want to move around the house or check out some other area, ask for permission first.
- If you need to go to the bathroom, ask for directions. Remember to keep the bathroom clean at all times.
- Feel free to ask about photos and other decorations that can be a good topic for conversation.
- If you land upon a sensitive topic, such as the death of a friend, give your sincerest apologies and move on.
- If you are meeting someone for the first time, it is a good idea to keep topics light and open-ended. This way you can gauge if the person may react positively or otherwise towards certain topics.

- Do not gossip with the person or you might give the impression of being someone who can't be trusted.
- When it is time to leave, give your warmest thanks and say it has been a pleasure getting to know them or it has been a pleasure to share such a lovely evening with them. Shake hands and look at the person in the eye again as you bid farewell.

Some extra things to do if you are going to stay over at someone else's house are:
- Wake up or get up a little bit after or at the same time as the house owner. If necessary, ask them what time they wake up. If they're still sleeping it wouldn't be nice to hear someone else's footsteps around the house. Don't get up if your hosts are still sleeping, if you can't sleep longer try doing something that's not going to make any noise that could disturb your hosts.
- If you need anything, ask for it. There's no worse feeling as a host than knowing your guests weren't comfortable or didn't have a good time.
- Ask your hosts about their schedule and tell them about yours. This will help them plan activities without disrupting the ones you have already planned for yourself.
- Bring your own toiletries such as toothbrush, deodorant, shampoo and razor. If you forget any of these, you can ask your host if they have some that you can use or if they could drive you to a supermarket to get the things you've forgotten. Don't expect your host to have everything you need in their home.
- Tell them about any food preferences or allergies that you might have. If you ask for a specific food and they get it for you, you should make sure to eat it.
- Leave everything clean such as the bathroom or kitchen if you use them. Make your bed in the morning and leave the room clean.

- Help them with responsibilities around the house such as cleaning or cooking. If possible, do your own laundry.
- As a thank you, give your hosts a gift or take them out for dinner or entertainment. They have gone out of their way to accommodate you.
- Once you have arrived back home, send a thank you card, call or text your hosts to thank them for having you.

Don't be afraid to ask for small things, relax and enjoy your stay. Always try to be in a good mood and be grateful for what they give you. You might even be able to return the favor if they visit your city.

WORK-RELATED ETIQUETTE

There is a social element to most offices, so observe the protocol and remember that your behaviour will affect your future. Once people see you misbehave at work, it is difficult to get that visual out of their minds. This is why it is essential to get off on the right foot from the beginning. However, if you've already made some mistakes, people tend to forget over time, but you'll need to be patient and maintain good manners, even when people make comments about your old ways.

Most working people spend more waking hours at the office than at home with their family, so it's worth establishing and maintaining solid business relationships, no matter how difficult it might be. You should develop trust in each other or the work will be more difficult. Remember you are all working towards the same goal. If you have a problem with one of your coworkers, take it to HR but never talk it out in front of other people. This takes hard work but it can pay off in the future, making the difference between career success and failure.

Teamwork
Companies typically expect their employees to be good team workers and to do their jobs to the betterment of the whole. This means that you must accept your position in the overall order of the corporation. Remember that every job is important or the company wouldn't spend money on salaries, benefits and training. All employees, regardless of their position, should feel free to greet each other in passing. Don't be afraid to say good morning or good afternoon in the hallway. If you are in the restroom at the same time, keep the greeting short and allow the other person his or her own privacy.

How to treat your boss or supervisors

Truth is, you should treat all people with the same amount of respect just because they're people and you're educated and classy. Of course, it is a whole different thing to deal with a manager than with a coworker that's on your level, professionally speaking.

Supervisors, as they are now called, typically set the tone for the department and determine whether the environment is formal or more relaxed. You should always address your supervisor by his or her surname, such as Mr. or Mrs. Smith, unless you are asked to do otherwise. Let them take the lead on invitations. Never air complaints about your job, coworkers, or the company during personal time with your supervisor. Schedule an appointment during business hours to keep it on a professional level. If you are a supervisor yourself you should never discuss your professional or personal problems with subordinates. Complaints should always go up in the chain of command. In cases where the supervisor shows bad manners, maintain your dignity and proper etiquette.

How to treat your coworkers

If you are new at your job, take some time to observe how everyone acts. Test the waters and avoid commenting on topics that you don't fully understand. Once you have established yourself as a congenial team player, go ahead and let your personality shine through. Do your best to cause a good first impression as they are very difficult to change. You should learn a few things about your coworkers such as their names and titles, company acronyms that apply to your job and task and reporting responsibilities. If someone asks for volunteers to assist on a project, be the one to step up and offer help. When the moment comes and you need others' assistance they will be more likely to cooperate with you. People will appreciate your hard work and commitment but avoid patting yourself on the back too often as you might come across as a bragger.

How to maintain a good relationship with your coworkers
- Never repeat anything negative.
- Avoid participating in office gossip.
- When handling cash, have another coworker present.
- Never call a coworker "sweetie", "honey" or any other term of endearment, even in jest. It may come across as sexual harassment.
- Never take credit for a coworker's idea or work.
- Always praise your coworkers for a job well done.
- If you want something, remember to say "Please" and "Thank you".
- If you carpool with coworkers, set rules for the trip on the way to and from work.
- Show respect for your coworkers during business hours and also when you're out of work.

Dress code and other policies
Every office has their own dress code and it also varies in the levels of permissiveness of what you can or can't wear. In some offices, it might be okay for you to wear jeans while in others you're expected to wear either formal trousers or skirts. Some companies have their dress code written in a policy handbook while others don't. If you aren't sure how to dress for work, ask someone. Also look around to see what others are wearing. You can usually tell how relaxed a dress code is by looking at your coworkers. Business casual attire can vary from denim to formal trousers.
Many offices have adopted additional policies to accommodate issues that are specific to their needs. You may have to deal with tight security measures, allergies that require fragrance-free zones and rules about eating or drinking at your desk. These policies have been put in place for a reason, so you should follow them at all times not only for respect for the company and your coworkers but also for the risk of being reprimanded.

Clients and Guests

You are likely to find yourself in the position of interacting with clients or guests in your workplace. Smile, introduce yourself while looking at them directly and ask if and how you can help them. Offer something to make them more comfortable while they wait. This can be a seat, coffee or water, a magazine or even food. In that moment, you are the face of the company, be sure to make a good impression.

SOCIAL MEDIA ETIQUETTE

As the use of the internet continues to expand into every aspect of people's lives, from emailing and social networking to scheduling job interviews and doctors appointments, many of us have become complacent, formed bad habits, and tossed proper etiquette aside. This is unfortunate and may create problems if we don't learn and apply a few basic rules. Internet etiquette is essential in a civilised work environment or personal relationship. Remember you can know everything about a person just by going through their social media. Of course, people try to show the best version of themselves in social media and that's okay. The way I see it is as platforms to show the best moments of your life or other special things you enjoy with your friends and loved ones, be careful with who you accept and give access to your pictures and information.

Be nice
The first rule of internet etiquette is to be kind and courteous. Never flame or rant in a public forum, not even when using an anonymous account. Show respect for the opinion of others, even if you don't agree with them, and refrain from name-calling. Avoid gossiping or saying anything negative about others. Remember that once you put it out there, it's going to be there forever. You might erase a post or message but the other person has already seen it and can even screenshot it and show other people. Never say anything negative about your company, your former company, your boss, coworkers, friends or family. You never know what may end up being forwarded, whether it's intentional or an accidental slip of the finger on the "send" button. If you are unsure about anything you've typed, hold it in draft mode and read it later before sending the email or posting the status update. Doing

otherwise could jeopardise your opportunity for a promotion, or worse, cost you your current job. Being nice includes avoiding cyber bullying. Think about how you would feel if someone said whatever you just typed about you. If you find it the least bit disturbing, delete it. Cyber bullying may lead to disaster if a despondent person perceives he or she is being threatened.

Learn internet acronyms
As communication over the internet explodes, so does the use of acronyms. Learn what they mean so you won't misunderstand messages and comments. If you don't know what an acronym means, you can always google it.

Keep Messages and Posts Brief
Most people use the internet to save time, so honor that and keep messages as brief as possible. Unless, of course you are talking to friends or people you have more connection with. If you have more to say, try breaking it up into smaller topics. This will force you to be more organised and enable the reader to digest the information in a more orderly manner.

Don't shout
Avoid using all caps in any emails or posts. Some people think that keeping the caps lock button on for the entire message will make it easier to read, while it actually does the opposite. It is not only more difficult to read but it also comes across as if you were shouting, which is perceived as rude.

Use discretion
Whether you are sending emails, instant messaging, commenting on Facebook, adding images to Snapchat, or posting a message to your blog, you need to remember that anything you put on the internet can be there forever. Even if you remove the material, someone may have

copied or saved it. One rule of thumb many people use is to never post anything you wouldn't like your parents or boss to see.

Protect personal information
Since anything you post on the Internet is out there for everyone to look at, avoid adding anything personal. This includes your address, phone number, credit or debit card number, social security number, driver's license or passport information. You don't want this information to be easily accesible for identity thieves, burglars or predators.

Obey copyright laws
Never copy someone else's work and post it as your own. It is against copyright law because it is considered stealing. It is always a good idea to ask for permission before quoting anyone, but that isn't always possible. If you want to quote someone, keep the quote short, cite the source, and add a link to the complete written work.

Before you click "send"
It is always a good idea to reread anything you type before clicking the "send" button. If you have time, step away for a few minutes and come back to it with fresh eyes. If not, check your spelling, grammar, and tone of the message one last time before sending. If it is late at night and you are extremely tired, it is probably best to wait until the next morning. You can save most messages and posts in draft mode.

Help others
If someone appears to be new to the internet, offer your assistance. Share information on proper etiquette, send them a link to a list of acronyms and emoticons, and offer to answer any questions until they get a hang of it. If you see that someone has posted something inappropriate, let

him or her know privately. Never do anything to publicly embarrass anyone you know online.

Alcohol
Alcohol and social media don't mix well. Avoid publishing pictures or status updates while under the influence of alcohol, drugs or strong emotions such as anger or stress. It is better to avoid social media altogether than to regret publishing something embarrassing or potentially damaging to your career. Remember, once it's out there and people have seen it there's no way to undo it. Try not to appear in pictures if you're drunk, you never know who could see this picture. Publishing this content won't seem like such a good idea the next day.

Pictures
For social gatherings, it is better to take the pictures on the early stages of the party where everybody looks good. Always pick the picture in which everyone looks good, they'll thank you for that. Before publishing any picture you should ask the other people in it if it's okay to do so and if they approve the picture. It's not very nice to publish a picture in which your friend looks anything short of decent, even if you look totally stunning! It's not the right thing to do and if you must publish that picture just crop your friend, I'm sure he or she will appreciate it.

Status updates
You must know your audience, sometimes you might think it is cool to post something when in reality it just isn't and your friends might react negatively. If you're unsure about whether to post it or not, it's probably better off the internet.

Funny posts
We all have that one friend who loves tagging us in the "like this if you're a hoe" or generally politically incorrect posts. I won't say I don't enjoy these posts because they

never fail to make me laugh, but it's a smarter technique to have your friend send them over WhatsApp rather than showing the whole Facebook community as this might backfire and could be offensive or embarrassing to your family members.

RELIGIOUS ETIQUETTE

Throughout your life, you are very likely to be invited to many religious celebrations such as weddings or quinceañeras and even to gatherings for the passing of a loved one. Always respect other people's religion and beliefs, they're just as important as yours are for yourself. Don't judge other religions even if you can't comprehend their beliefs. Whether you are invited to catholic masses or christian services you should always behave appropriately and respectfully.

If a friend or someone you know invites you to one of these you should always thank them for their invitation, whether you are going or not. You shouldn't be offended by said invitation as they are most likely coming from a good place. Most people invite you when they want to celebrate a special occasion and you attending expresses your support, even if you don't share the same beliefs.

Be sure to know which dress code you should follow when attending the ceremonies, in some occasions you might have to cover your hair, shoulders or legs out of respect. If you are unsure about how to dress, you can ask the friend who invited you if you should dress in any particular way.

If someone is inviting you to go with them as a way to change your religion or spiritual beliefs, kindly decline and explain you are happy with your position and would prefer if they didn't try to change them. If they keep pushing maybe it is time to start distancing yourself as it's not respectful from their part.

If you're uncomfortable attending a religious celebration that doesn't align with yours (or your religion is against attending other religious gatherings) just say no, it'll be a lot better than suffering the stress for around an hour. I'm sure your friends or whoever invited you will understand if you politely decline their invitation.

CONCLUSION AND SUMMARY

As long as we share certain values in life, we will intentionally or unintentionally exercise some or other form of etiquette, either in a rough way, or in a more sophisticated manner. No matter what we do, we can never live without etiquette being a very integral part of our lives. It is up to us though, to refine our mannerism so that it portrays the values we carry in our heart.

Etiquette is pure and purposeful.
Once you realise what part etiquette plays in your life, you can start to work on your own etiquette and before long, you will start to see positive results.
Unknown to most of us, we are judged by others on how we treat them and how they view us through our manner, in other words, depending on the etiquette we follow.
In conclusion, etiquette makes us human and distinguishes us from all other forms of life. So everyone should accept the responsibility of learning how to follow the standard etiquette of their society.

Summarising the most important lessons of this book,
- Don't do to other what you wouldn't like them to do to you.
- Be considerate.
- Be kind.
- If you are unsure about how you should act, ask yourself how would you feel if you were the person interacting with you.
- Choose your words carefully.
- Respect every person you interact with.
- Always be courteous and grateful.
- Take special care of your appearance and cleanness.
- Try to make everyone you meet feel good.
- When in doubt, mimic other people that you know are a good reference.

- Always follow the dress code and policy handbook if there's one.
- If you are having someone over, do as much as you can to make them feel comfortable.
- If you are visiting someone, bring a gift and thank them for having you afterwards.
- Offer your help to people in need.
- Don't post anything you wouldn't like your family or boss to see.
- Don't do anything that makes you feel uncomfortable.
- If you don't have anything nice to say, say nothing.
- If you must say something, there is a proper way to do so.

Education goes a long way and it shines through when you have proper etiquette.

WORDS FROM THE AUTHOR

Hello, nice to meet you! My name is Valentina Palermo and I have been attending etiquette courses and conferences ever since I was 15. Even though etiquette is only one of my many interests it has to be one of the skills that has been the most useful for me. I'm currently studying business administration at university and making connections is one of the most important skills you can have since you have to do a lot of networking at all times. Etiquette has allowed me to reach better opportunities and I hope it continues to do so just as I hope it helps you reach your own goals as well.

Thank you for taking the time to read this book, I hope it was a pleasant read but most importantly, one that has added value to your life.

Sincerely yours,
Valentina

Printed in Great Britain
by Amazon